Self-Discipline in Difficult Times

Pressing Ahead (or Not) When Your World Turns Upside Down

By Martin Meadows

Download Another Book for Free

As thanks for buying my book, I want to offer you another, completely free: *Grit: How to Keep Going When You Want to Give Up.*

In *Grit*, I'll give you some pointers on how to stick to your goals using proven methods from peak performers and science. In addition to receiving *Grit*, as my newsletter subscriber you'll also get bonus content, limited offers, and updates about my new books.

Here's the link to sign up:

https://www.profoundselfimprovement.com/dt

Table of Contents

Prologue

As I type these words in April 2020, the world is experiencing the worst crisis in the modern history. Virtually every single country across the globe is locked down: poor or rich, big or small. Levels of anxiety are through the roof as we're forced to adapt to a new way of living, in a constant state of worry about the repercussions.

To say that staying disciplined in these times is difficult would be a grand understatement. According to a *Forbes* article on how Americans are coping with the quarantine, alcohol sales were up 55% in the week ending March 21, 2020. Marijuana sales in states where it's legal soared, too. A popular pornography website saw a 11.6% increase in traffic. Video streaming of non-adult content has doubled. With panic-stricken shoppers stocking up on highly processed shelf-stable items, people are eating more than ever before and gaining even more weight (the phenomenon has been dubbed the "quarantine 15," with the number indicating pounds).

But we don't need a global crisis for our worlds to turn upside down. Self-discipline, motivation, and good habits are the last things we think about when we lose a loved one, when we lose a job, when our business goes bankrupt, when our heart is broken, when we face a disease or our loved one is struggling with one, or even when we face one minor setback too many and just can't find it in us to keep going.

As a self-help author *and* reader, I'm tired of cheap, often inconsiderate motivational messages addressed at those whose life foundations have been rocked to the core by an unexpected crisis. Over the next pages, I don't plan to berate you for being weak or lazy, or belittle your problems, whatever they may be. Instead, I want to discuss when and how we can press ahead when the pressure seems insurmountable.

Unlike my other books, which are heavy on research, this book, and other books in my "Self-Help Essays" series, are opinion pieces. If you're looking for a more evidence-based examination of mental resilience, read my book *From Failure to Success* or

Grit (which you get for free when you sign up for my newsletter).

If you're ready for a quick, personal, and hopefully comforting read, let's turn the page and start at the beginning: what to do in the immediate aftermath of your world turning upside down.

Chapter 1: The World Is Upside Down—What Now?

I would not wish on anyone to receive the phone call I received that fateful September night, right after I landed overseas. While I was crossing the ocean, oblivious to it all, a family member had died suddenly at the age of fifty-four.

My heart was broken. My sense of security was destroyed. I, a person everyone calls cool, calm, and collected, had panic attacks. Obsessive thoughts tormented me day and night, as I replayed the worst moments over and over again.

As I write these words, I'm better—on the other side of the pain, if you will, but not the same as before. And neither will anyone who has ever experienced a negative event that fundamentally changes your world.

You don't think about much else when you're shaken to the core. Anyone who tells you to "snap out of it" can at best hope to be ignored, if you still have a shred of self-control left, and at worst, if you're unhinged, be met with violent words or actions.

To tell a griever to look to the future might as well be criminal. They didn't plan to have their hearts broken, their dreams wiped away, their sense of normalcy pulverized. Days, weeks, months, and sometimes even years are needed to process what happened. There's no timeline for any of this, no convenient "stages" that you go through in a linear order until you recover. Few people, if any, are capable of processing dramatic changes overnight and getting back to work right away.

Is there any hope to be had during those dark times, anything that you can do to improve your hopeless situation?

As I pondered on this topic, I came to one key conclusion: nothing can be said or done to make things better if you've just suffered an earth-shattering change in your life, particularly the loss of a loved one. The only thing that "helped" me was to revert to survival level, focusing on my basic needs alone: somehow get sufficient sleep, try to eat healthy, and attempt to move just a little bit. You're dealing with the immediate aftermath of what happened—there's no need to worry about anything else. The only thing that matters is to survive.

There's no motivational speaker in the world, no piece of advice, no book that's going to make things right. I can't stress this enough: I'm not qualified to talk about heart-breaking grief, and I don't think that any self-help work can assist during the initial, hardest stage.

Whether you decide to seek professional help or rely on your loved ones for support during these trying times, don't let anyone make you feel guilty for "dropping the ball" (you're not dropping anything; you're desperately trying not to lose your sanity) or force you to rush your recovery. Let your brain process what happened, no matter how much time it takes. If you're still feeling completely overwhelmed, you may return to this book when you feel a little bit more in control.

Mitigating Less Destructive Personal Challenges

Now that we've acknowledged how certain hardships in life are irreparable and require staying away from any kind of self-help literature, let's move on to the main focus of this book: hardships that can wreak havoc in our lives, but that aren't as damaging as losing a loved one or other events with a similar emotional intensity.

Examples of less destructive, somewhat reversible, but still intense hardships include losing a job, your business going bankrupt, a breakup, a global recession, or struggling with a non-fatal disease that can be managed with medication. All of these difficulties may turn our worlds upside down—I'm not denying their impact—but while a parent can't replace a child they've just lost, a person who lost a job has a chance to find a new one.

If you can easily *identify* potential upsides of your crisis, you're most likely dealing with a hardship that this book can help you recover from. Just to be clear: I'm not asking you to *believe* that the situation is good for you and that you should snap out of it right now. I'm only asking you to acknowledge that there *might* be possible upsides.

Now that it's clear that certain misfortunes are beyond the scope of this book, let's turn our focus toward problems that we can learn to control.

Protecting Yourself From Yourself

Mitigating the destructive effects of unforeseen, overwhelming difficulties starts with clearing your head. Nothing good has ever come out of decisions made in an emotionally charged state.

Insulting your boss for firing you? Not the smartest way to protect your reputation in the industry. Heading to a night club, drinking yourself silly, and sleeping with a random stranger after a breakup? Not a responsible choice in your fragile mental state. Publicly snapping at a big client who just decided to pull out of a once-in-a-lifetime contract? Not the best path to ensuring the long-term survival of your business.

Might you feel tempted to engage in these behaviors? Of course—just like everyone who has ever experienced hard times. I've been there as well, snapping at friends who couldn't empathize the way I wanted them to and engaging in reckless driving—thankfully, on empty roads at night, though I'm still not proud of it—as I dealt with a dark period in my life and didn't care if I crashed into a tree.

What do you do when it feels as if someone else—someone irresponsible—is at the steering wheel of your life? At all costs, you create distance, literal or figurative, between you and the problem. Stressed out, you have only a sliver of self-discipline left—use it to create some distance and avoid making a bad situation even worse.

When faced with an overwhelming temptation to snap at your spouse for trying to be helpful when you know it won't help, just take a big, long breath and leave the room. Your business might be bankrupt, but it doesn't mean that your marriage needs to go down the drain, too.

Sleep on it ("it" being something you might regret forever, like a public post on social media) and decide if you still want to do it the next day, with a clear head. How many reputations could have been saved by simply consulting one's pillow?

When countless setbacks get the best of you and you want to destroy your half-finished project, take a walk or call a friend to cool yourself down. It's not worth it to let yourself lose control only to realize later that one snap decision destroyed weeks or months of work.

The goal isn't to deny that you're going through something hard but to recognize that you can control—to a certain extent—your emotional response. First and foremost, you do it through creating distance. This way, you avoid letting one hardship create cascading issues that will further impact your life and make recovery even harder.

I have a simple policy: whenever I struggle with hardships or even just wake up in a bad mood, I warn my girlfriend about it. Not because I'm looking for a fight and want to make things even worse, but precisely because I want to avoid any confrontations in which I might not be able to control myself. In the same way, I try to stay away from certain people, places, and activities that might tempt me to turn a bad situation into a worse one. Again, this is not to deny that I'm dealing with something hard but to make sure that one difficulty doesn't turn into multiple problems I could have easily avoided. This is possible thanks to self-awareness and a modicum of restraint.

This is the key takeaway from this chapter: in the immediate aftermath of a crisis, use your last shreds of self-discipline to get yourself away from the source of suffering. Nothing else matters—just get away.

THE WORLD IS UPSIDE DOWN—
WHAT NOW? QUICK RECAP

1. If you've just experienced an earth-shattering crisis, don't worry about motivation, self-discipline, or habits. Your primary focus for now is your survival: focus on your most basic needs and disregard the rest. Now is not the time to think ahead—it's the time to focus on what you need at the very moment to survive this awful period.

2. If you don't have to think hard to identify potential upsides of your hardships, then this book may help you recover. If the mere thought of such upsides offends you, no piece of advice is relevant to you at the moment. Stay away from self-help literature and get support from your loved ones, or seek professional help.

3. The most critical mitigation strategy to employ in the immediate aftermath of a tough situation is to use your dwindling reserves of self-control to put some distance between you and the problem.

Chapter 2: Managing Your Coping Mechanisms

We all react in different ways to hardships. Some isolate themselves, seeking solitude to process what happened. Others surround themselves with as many people as possible to get support. Some binge eat junk food. Others refuse to eat. Some spend entire days watching TV and sleeping. Others fill their days with activity, often to a compulsive level.

Let's discuss some common coping mechanisms and how to use them in a balanced way.

Rest

Hardships put immense stress on our bodies. Little things you wouldn't even have noticed before can now throw you off balance. What used to be an easy task becomes a giant challenge as you struggle to pay attention, your mind occupied by all the what-ifs, regrets, and worries.

This is why rest is a key coping strategy when you're dealing with the aftermath of a big crisis.

Motivational coaches would like you to believe that you can push through any obstacle and persevere no matter what. And you can—but not if you don't allow your body to rest. This is your starting point and by far the most important coping mechanism before you even consider other methods.

It sounds obvious that we need to rest when we're under too much pressure, yet when faced with a big crisis, we often behave differently.

Instead of letting ourselves pause for a few days or a few weeks, we immediately seek solutions, bombard ourselves with negative thoughts, blame ourselves for what happened, deny that it happened, or outright punish ourselves by inflicting self-harm.

These are all natural responses. We might not be able to control them easily, but we can consciously focus on self-care over self-hate. First and foremost, this means not feeling guilty that you aren't being productive. That is the *most important message* of this book: you can't expect to successfully handle the consequences of a big crisis until you first get yourself in the right mental state. This means healing yourself, not hurting yourself through self-guilt.

That brings us to self-care, which starts with rest. To identify what helps you recover the most, think of all the places, people, or activities that make you calm. How would you describe your most relaxing environment? What is it that makes it so tranquil?

Nature is the most soothing environment for me—swimming in the ocean, taking a walk through the forest, enjoying the views from the top of a mountain. This is my definition of a stress-free land, a place where my brain can get a respite from the hardships tormenting it. This is where I head when I want to heal myself.

What's your environment? How can you get yourself there? If that's impossible, how can you recreate at least certain features of it in your daily life? For example, you might not be able to travel to your favorite vacation destination, but perhaps you can browse through some old pictures or videos. Stuck at home during the lockdown, I couldn't surf, but at least I could lie down, stare into the blue sky, and visualize I was in the water. Anything that calms you down even just a little is helpful as you try to rebuild your life in the new world.

As you focus on recovery, be mindful of healthy balance. Strapped for self-discipline, in a negative mental state, you may *temporarily* let go of your high standards. This is understandable and expected. However, be cautious not to use personal crises as excuses to sabotage your goals. Don't forget that there *is* life after the crisis; try not to let your coping mechanism create new, lasting problems.

Watching TV series, playing video games, or engaging in any other similar activity that helps you escape your problems can be a restorative experience. I don't think these are bad, per se. However, if taken too far—to the point that they're all you do the entire day for weeks on end—you may end up in a vicious cycle of inactivity that will only worsen your mental state.

A few days might not be dangerous, but spending several weeks doing nothing but binge-watching TV shows can lead to negative habits that will not only make you feel worse, but will also threaten your long-term goals. Again, this doesn't mean that you can't watch TV during your recovery phase—just try to keep it under control as a *temporary* self-soothing measure. To avoid developing an unhealthy, monotonous routine that will harm your mental state, mix it up with other activities. Meditate. Write in a journal. Sit in the sun. Take a nap. Practice yoga. Talk with a friend. Read a book. Listen to music. Exercise.

Similarly, if eating your favorite foods gets you through tough times, that's a helpful tool. But if taken to the extreme through binge eating, you may gain so much weight that once you recover from the current crisis, you'll face the prospect of weeks or months of dieting. Again, this doesn't mean that you can't or shouldn't comfort yourself with food *temporarily* and *within limits*.

With limited physical activity during the lockdown—and emotional eating serving as one of my primary self-soothing strategies—my weight increased every day. After two weeks of seeing higher and higher numbers on the scale, I decided it was time to stop comforting myself with food. I hit my hard limit—I realized that if I kept going, my *temporary* coping mechanism would lead to new long-term problems. I started counting calories and shifted to other coping mechanisms that didn't threaten my waist size (one of which was reading fiction). My weight started dropping right away, and my two weeks of self-soothing with food didn't lead to lasting diet-related willpower challenges.

To further mitigate negative long-term effects of *temporarily* letting yourself go, consider healthier alternatives. Indulge in dried fruits instead of candy, even if it's only one dried fruit per ten candies. Prepare homemade pizza instead of buying a highly processed frozen one, even if it's only once a week. Eat sweets that are lower in sugar and higher in fiber, even if they're still caloric. All these little acts of self-discipline won't cost you much, but they'll still help you keep *some* self-control.

Also, avoid supermarkets when you're hungry, thirsty, or feeling particularly stressed out. My period of lockdown overeating was fueled by seeking comfort in supermarket aisles I should have stayed well away from.

Seek Support (or Solitude)

As an introvert, I seek solitude when I face a hardship. Extroverts may seek support immediately and talk over their problems with friends or family members. Ambiverts, people in the middle of the spectrum, may lean either way depending on the problem at hand.

Whatever your coping mechanism, cultivate balance and be open to shifting your strategy.

For those seeking solitude, excess isolation may lead to strained relationships, an inability to look at the problem from a different perspective (the kind that a friend may offer), or paradoxically, feeling lonely—even though it was your decision to avoid people. There's nothing wrong with temporary withdrawal if that's what you need. Be mindful of potential long-term consequences, though, and don't be afraid to change your mind and seek support when solitude isn't helping you anymore. It can be a tough pill to swallow for hardcore introverts. But from one introvert to another, believe me—we can't exist without other people, and sometimes they offer the only way out of a crisis.

For those who seek external support right away, be aware that in the end, nobody can solve your problems for you. Eventually you may need some time alone, too. Everyone has a different perspective—which is valuable—but because of that, everyone also looks at your problem through their own lens, which may not be in line with what you believe is the right thing for you. For example, when I debated some tough business decisions after a setback, I received a lot of advice that took into account pure numbers only. It was understandable coming from a person with an engineering background. It didn't match what I felt internally about the situation, though. It was solitude that helped me make the right decision.

Support as a recovery tool isn't meant to force you to seek solutions and take action. Spend time with other people to forget about your hardships and to feel that you can count on them, not to let them convince you to make important decisions when you aren't ready yet.

Engage in Physical Activity

The body has countless mechanisms we don't control that affect how we feel. One of these is endorphins—feel-good hormones that are released during physical activity. Even when you feel down, you can't consciously force the body not to release them. Exercise will make you temporarily feel better, whether you like it or not. This makes it a useful coping strategy.

No matter how bad the situation is (within the limits we addressed in the first chapter), breaking a little sweat will help you enter a more resourceful state of mind. For best results, choose exercise that you enjoy, ideally in nature, and keep intensity manageable to avoid injuries. Avoid putting your body under too much physical stress through compulsive exercise or imprudent risk-taking, which is more likely to inflict self-harm than encourage self-care.

Engage in Restorative Productivity

When you suffer from a difficult crisis or a huge setback in life, your default response, as a person dedicated to personal development, might be to press ahead and try to fix things right away. *Looking* for solutions is okay, but *taking action* is usually not.

Of course, if you're facing the possibility of your business going bankrupt or losing your job, you'll fight to avert a crisis. But if your business has already gone bankrupt or you've already lost your job, immediately starting a new venture or seeking new employment might not be the most ideal solution. We've already explained why: to make good decisions, you need to recover, gain some distance, cool down, and find a more objective perspective. It's rare that we can make good decisions in a vulnerable state.

In the meantime, you can regain some confidence through what I like to call "restorative productivity"—working on tasks of little importance that nonetheless will make you feel productive and help restore some normalcy. This can be something as simple as reorganizing your kitchen, cleaning your house, throwing away old junk, or removing unnecessary apps from your phone. You can also cope through engaging in simple DIY tasks like building a raised garden bed, painting a room, or fixing something. Anything that's a relatively easy task and is unrelated to your hardship is fair game.

Restorative productivity helps cultivate a sense of progress, which in turn helps maintain hope that things will get better. After all, if you're improving in *something*, eventually you can improve the bad situation, too, can't you?

During the lockdown, the biggest challenge for me, as well as for millions of people around the world, was to stay at home. I go crazy whenever I can't spend time outdoors, so an extended period of time during which I was forced to forgo visiting my favorite places and participating in my favorite sports was absolute misery for me. Each day, I was getting weaker and more restless, worrying that I would lose all the progress I had made in my fitness goals, missing the nature that always made me feel so good, even when I was having a bad day.

One strategy that helped me stay sane was cultivating a sense of progress in fitness areas I wasn't good at. One of these was body flexibility. I started a new thirty-day yoga series (the free thirty-day "Home" series from Yoga with Adriene, which you can find on YouTube). Even though I found it hard to begin, after a few days I noticed some progress. Improvements in my yoga practice fueled my resolve to keep going, offering a sliver of hope that there were some fitness gains I could still achieve despite being stuck at home. Yoga couldn't replace my favorite activities, but it did help me maintain some positivity, which was key to avoid losing my mind in these difficult times.

Note that restorative productivity is *optional*. Don't let yourself feel guilty when you aren't productive all day long during your recovery period. Your main job is to get better; whether you accomplish this through any of the strategies offered in this chapter or something else, it doesn't matter.

Do whatever you need to do to rest, clear your mind, and eventually regain control over your mental state. The more focus you put on recovery now, the faster you'll be able to bounce back.

MANAGING YOUR COPING MECHANISMS: QUICK RECAP

1. Rest is the most important coping mechanism, a starting point for recovery from a crisis. Focus on self-care by identifying what makes you feel good and engaging in these activities until you feel better. Make sure that you maintain balance, though: self-soothing with TV series, video games, or your favorite foods can be helpful, but you don't want to develop an unhealthy addiction. Mix things up, consider healthier alternatives, and remember that your period of recovery is a temporary measure and you don't want to cause new long-term problems.

2. Depending on what you need most at the moment, seek support or solitude. In both cases, proper balance is key. Solitude can help recharge your batteries, particularly if you're an introvert, but don't be afraid of seeking support when you feel lonely. In contrast, seeking support and other perspectives can be helpful, but don't expect others to solve your problems for you.

3. Physical activity can be a great ally on your journey toward recovery. Make sure that you engage in your favorite sports without putting your body under too much stress. Again, you want self-care, not self-destruction.

4. Engage in restorative productivity—working on projects and solving problems of little importance. This way, you'll regain some self-confidence, feel productive, and cultivate a sense of hope that things can, and eventually will, get better.

5. Don't feel guilty when you aren't productive during your recovery period. Your main job is to get better—this is a tough job in itself.

Chapter 3: When You're Ready to Dig Yourself Out

As you focus on daily recovery, eventually a day comes when you tell yourself that you feel good enough to start digging yourself out. You might not be healed entirely yet, and the trauma might still be there, but you're strong enough to bounce back. You're ready to try again (look for a new job, start a new business, or open your heart to a new relationship) or pivot to something else (switch your career, move to a different city, or try a different strategy altogether to get what you want).

In this chapter we'll go through three strategies you can use to begin the process and slowly, but steadily, get yourself back on track.

Reframe Your Crisis

In simple words, reframing is the process of changing the meaning of what happened to you. I like how Tony Robbins puts it: things happen *for* us instead of *to* us. Of course, just to reiterate the main point from the first chapter, this only applies when talking about hardships that may have a silver lining and are relatively easy to reframe.

At first, you may be skeptical that there's anything of value in losing a job, your heart getting broken, your business going bankrupt, or you developing a chronic disease, even if you know examples of people who have found meaning in their hardships. That's why we dedicated the first two chapters to biding your time, letting yourself adapt to the new world and recover from the initial shock. Now that you're starting to think about rebuilding, reframing makes sense, as you won't react with such (understandable) skepticism.

There's an old story about a farmer and his son. Through hard work, they saved enough money to buy an old horse to pull their cart for them. Their neighbors told them, "You're so lucky to have a horse," to which the farmer replied, "Maybe so, maybe not. We'll see."

One day, the horse ran away and the neighbors exclaimed, "Your horse ran away, what a terrible misfortune!" The farmer replied, "Maybe so, maybe not. We'll see."

A few days later, the horse returned home with a few wild mares. The neighbors were ecstatic: "You're so lucky! Your horse is back and now you're rich." The farmer replied, "Maybe so, maybe not. We'll see."

A few days later, as the farmer's son was trying to break one of the mares, she threw him to the ground and he broke his leg. The neighbors pitied the farmer: "Your son broke his leg, what a terrible misfortune!" The farmer replied, "Maybe so, maybe not. We'll see."

As his son was recovering from the injury, soldiers came to the village and took away all the able-bodied young men to fight in the war. The farmer's son was spared. The neighbors said, "Your boy was spared, you're so lucky!" The farmer replied, "Maybe so, maybe not. We'll see."

The ending of the story might be abrupt, but it's abrupt for a reason—to indicate the cyclical nature of our hardships. It could end right there, on the cycle before, or a hundred cycles later. Now, in my mind, this story doesn't mean that whatever fortunate thing happens in our lives always precedes a disaster. Rather, it's meant to teach that we can interpret every event in our lives in two ways.

As I developed a serious muscle strain that caused intense pain with every movement, I couldn't find anything good in it. I was getting weaker. I was missing my favorite sports. I was forgetting all the new skills I'd learned in surfing. And of course, I was growing spiteful and frustrated. Why me? Why was it taking so long to heal? How long would it take to regain what I lost, let alone start progressing again? I eventually recovered, but I wasn't happy with all the time that I'd lost, nor did I see much value in the injury.

Then, a year later, I felt a similar twinge of pain. This time—thanks to my past experience—I didn't ignore it. I stopped exercising right away and redirected all my attention toward stretching and recovery. Instead of suffering another down period of two months, I was healed within two weeks. The first time I developed the injury was a blessing in disguise—it taught me to better listen to my body and saved me from an immense amount of pain later on, perhaps even a more serious injury.

This is why I asked you in the first chapter to *think of*—but not necessarily to *believe*— that there may be something to be gained from your crisis. Of course, my injury might be nothing compared to your broken heart, lost job, bankrupted business, or divorce, or any other unpleasant situation in life, but the point still stands: eventual upside can be found in all of this.

If you're ready to think about your hardships from a more empowering perspective, sit down in a quiet room and ask yourself what you can learn from what happened.

A heartbreak can help you understand what kind of people you shouldn't date or how you need to improve yourself to make sure that your next relationship is the one you've been looking for your entire life. It might even teach you that staying single is at the moment better than seeking a new partner—a crisis in our personal life often helps us pinpoint what we want in life in general.

Setbacks in your professional life can help you avoid getting another job you don't like much, working for yet another dictatorial boss, or maybe help you realize that you don't want to get another job at all, and instead want to try your hand at entrepreneurship or an alternative lifestyle.

Non-fatal, manageable health disorders might forever be a source of pain in your life but they may also help you refocus on your health and avoid other, potentially nastier conditions later on. Hypertension or diabetes might be the wake-up call you need to finally develop healthier habits. An early warning in the form of these unpleasant conditions has saved countless lives.

Focus on What You Can Control

In the previous chapter, we talked about restorative productivity—engaging in tasks that help you temporarily forget about the source of your anguish as you process what happened. Now that you feel ready to begin anew, it's important to focus exclusively on what you can control, so as to avoid disappointment. Let me explain this with a few examples.

Imagine Kate, who lost her job a few weeks ago. Her boss didn't warn her beforehand, and she was fired through no fault of her own ("downsizing," her boss said). She needed some time off to recover and think about what was next—time she used to catch up with some favorite TV shows, cook some delicious homemade meals, spend time with friends, get sufficient sleep, and ask herself how she wanted her career to progress. Now, she's ready to look for a new job. Unfortunately, her phone is silent. To avoid disappointment, she needs to focus on what she can control: improving her resume, taking free courses online to improve her skills, or reaching out to old acquaintances who might help her out. How likely would she be to bounce back if all she was thinking about was the fact that nobody was inviting her to an interview?

Imagine George, who despite his best intentions to fix the situation, was publicly slandered by a disgruntled client. With his reputation destroyed and his hope in humanity undermined, it takes him over a year before he's ready to clear his name. But the past still haunts him: all it takes is a quick Google search to read that nasty, baseless piece of so-called "journalism" and make all of his potential clients back out. George can't control the search engine results, but he can preempt clients' reactions by acknowledging what happened, presenting his side of the story, and doing all he can to reduce the risk for a client and convince them to give him a chance. How likely would he be to bounce back if all he was thinking about was the unfairness of it all and the inability to remove the article?

Imagine Natasha, a yoga teacher who was diagnosed with a dangerous disease that required complicated surgery and a long period of recovery. Now that she's able to walk without pain, her body is still too frail for anything more than that—including yoga practice. With little money left, she's forced to close her yoga school. But instead of getting angry about her body taking so long to recover—something she can't control and most certainly can't rush—she decides that her recovery needs to continue in a different direction. She starts a YouTube channel in which she shares her spiritual discoveries. She might never be able to reopen her yoga school, but she isn't letting it stop her from helping her students and providing value to the yoga world.

Surf to Surf Tomorrow

After suffering from many injuries—and with hope, finally learning from them—I adopted a new rule that pertains not only to surfing, but also life in general: "surf to surf tomorrow." This philosophy is explained in the introduction of an excellent book on health for surfers, *Surf Survival*, written by Andrew Nathanson, Clayton Everline, and Mark Renneker. It goes as follows: "One of my main ground rules is to always surf to surf again tomorrow, no matter what that takes. As bad as today might seem, the sun will come up again tomorrow, we get to paddle back out once more, and we can start fresh all over."

When applied to recovering from major setbacks in life, it comes down to always leaving something in the tank, giving yourself that small margin in case things get too difficult to handle in your current vulnerable state. To rebuild and eventually thrive again, focus on incremental and sustainable daily improvements. You're only beginning to pick up the pieces. Your mental bandwidth might still be limited as your confidence is on wobbly legs, the trauma lurking in the back of your head.

Just like it doesn't make sense to begin your recovery from a major injury with a grueling workout, it doesn't make sense to overwhelm your brain as you're taking the first steps. Start small and take it from there. Add new tasks only when you're comfortable with what's already on your plate. Back off when you feel like there's too much on your shoulders.

There will be time to challenge yourself again, to hustle hard, to push with all your might if you're so inclined—but not today. Today, you're focused on sustainably rebuilding your life.

As you regain confidence, mental strength, and all the good habits that were in your life prior to the crisis, you're ready to progress to the final stage: building resiliency for inevitable future crises. This is what we'll cover in the penultimate chapter.

WHEN YOU'RE READY TO DIG YOURSELF OUT: QUICK RECAP

1. When you feel ready, reframe your source of suffering by giving it a new, empowering meaning. Open yourself to the lessons it may present or the hidden blessings it can offer as you rebuild your life.

2. Focus on what you can control. If you obsess about things over which you have no influence, you'll feel helpless, which in turn will sabotage any efforts you might have taken to bounce back.

3. Surf to surf tomorrow. Don't forget that as you're recovering, your mental bandwidth might still be limited. This means that this is not the right time to push yourself to the limit. Take things step by step, day by day, and always remember that the goal is to do things today in such a way that you can do them again tomorrow.

Chapter 4: Preparing for Future Challenges

As much as we would love for our lives to be devoid of suffering, disappointment, sadness, and horror, facing painful situations is inevitable. Now that you've recovered and feel ready to press ahead, grow, and enjoy life, consider adding to your regular schedule the practice of voluntary suffering.

I know what you're thinking: the last thing you need right now is to suffer again. However, letting in some suffering—on your own terms, at your own pace, and only to the level you accept—helps build mental resilience and helps you better cope with future unplanned hardships.

When I talk about voluntary suffering, I don't mean deliberately sabotaging your efforts or making bad decisions just to make your life harder—this makes no sense and serves no purpose. Instead, I refer to expanding your comfort zone, a psychological state in which you feel at ease, in control, and surrounded by things you consider familiar.

I used to be terrified of heights and open water. I found my comfort zone only at sea level, but not too close to the depths of the sea, either. As I started deliberately facing my fear of heights through rock climbing, hiking, flying in a hot-air balloon, and even skydiving, my comfort zone regarding heights expanded. My quality of life has improved, and now I can enjoy scenic views and try new activities without paralyzing fear.

The same thing happened with open water. First I learned how to swim well, then I started surfing, and eventually I even tried scuba diving. This might be a silly example, but if I were to randomly fall off a boat, I would be able to rescue myself without much panic—while the same scenario sans years of voluntary suffering might have ended in a drowning.

As I trained myself to overcome these fears, I also learned about myself, about how I react to stressful situations. For example, as I sat on the edge of a boat, about to try scuba diving for the first time in my life, I was so afraid that I almost gave up. However, I knew that I'd felt similar fear—and had been able to overcome it—as I tried multi-pitch climbing for the first time, or as I immersed myself in frigid water in the middle of winter. Based on my previous experiences, I knew that the longer I hesitated, the more difficult it would become to overcome fear. So I leaned back and let gravity do its work. I was still engulfed in fear the first few minutes in the water, but it slowly dissipated. Eventually, I relaxed and was able to enjoy the underwater scenery.

What I learned as I experienced voluntary suffering in sports helped me overcome business and personal problems, too. Dealing with the fear of heights made me more confident in general. Learning how to swim in harmony with the power of the ocean instead of fighting against it helped me accept other things I couldn't control in my life. Reaching the breaking point during a tough wilderness medicine survival course helped me gain humility, as I realized that I wasn't indestructible.

I didn't have to engage in any of those activities—nothing was forcing me to—but they all served as indispensable tools to strengthen my mental resilience. There's a fable of Aesop I love that succinctly explains the importance of voluntary suffering even when all is right in your life at the moment. It goes like this:

A wild boar was sharpening his tusks against a tree, when a fox came by and asked him why he was doing this. "I don't see the reason," remarked the fox. "There are neither hunters nor hounds in sight; in fact, right now I can't see any threat at all."

The boar replied, "True, but when danger does arise, I'll have other things on my mind than sharpening my weapons."

This is just like voluntary suffering—you prepare yourself for suffering before there's any sign of it. Let's learn from the boar and discuss ways in which *you* can expand your comfort zone and be better prepared for whatever life throws at you. I've grouped these into three general categories.

Experiencing Extreme Mental States

A disclaimer first: I'm not a doctor, nor do I have a medical background of any kind, and I do not recommend engaging in any of the following ideas until you talk with a professional.

One of the most effective ways to push your mental limits and train yourself to deal with hardships is to voluntarily experience extreme mental states. This can be done through a variety of methods.

One of them is fasting. In today's era of plenty, most people in a position to read this book (and by association, well off enough to afford food on the table every day) are more likely to overeat than to starve. Periodically exposing yourself to real hunger—going without food for at least twenty-four hours—is an excellent way to explore your mental limits.

My longest fast lasted for over three days. The experience not only strengthened my self-discipline, but also made me appreciate food more. I now also know that if I couldn't eat for a few days (something that may happen during a natural disaster or a wilderness expedition), I would be fine. There's a sense of freedom in this realization.

Cold showers, saunas, winter swimming, ice baths—all of these activities involve unpleasant, extreme temperatures that will test your mental and physical limits. Obviously, as with any other practice in voluntary suffering, don't do any of them to the point you hurt yourself.

Regular exposure to cold water has provided me with plenty of mental benefits, including the ability to press ahead when my body screams "no" (again, to reiterate: in a mindful and safe way). It has also, in a twisted way, given me the ability to enjoy suffering. The first minute in cold water is horrible; once you adapt, the feeling of accomplishment is heavenly.

As evidenced by my experiences with heights and open water, facing your fears, whatever they may be, will also put you in an extreme mental state. As your fear dissipates with each exposure, you'll be less afraid of future unplanned scary situations.

Voluntary everyday discomfort—such as kinds you can experience while wild camping, on a multiday hike, or anywhere away from civilization—is yet another strategy that, whether you're well prepared or not—is likely to make you experience some extreme mental states. Physical exhaustion, adverse weather conditions, the feeling that you can rely only on yourself—all of these experiences can toughen you up. Again, we don't do that to create trauma, but rather to see where our limits are and push our comfort zones a little bit further out.

If such extreme ideas don't speak to you, even something as simple as sleeping on the floor, eating bland food for a week, not spending any money on entertainment for a month, or leaving your phone at home as you go for a walk around the block can be a successful strategy in experiencing voluntary discomfort.

Questioning Dogmas

There are many unwritten rules on how to operate in our society. Most of them make sense, but some we follow only because "that's how it's done," even though we have no idea who established them and for what reason.

There's an old story of a young woman who served a pot roast. One of her friends enjoyed the dish so much that she asked for the recipe. Upon looking it over, the friend asked, "Why do you cut both ends off the roast?" The young woman replied, "I cut them because I learned this recipe from my mom, and that was the way she had always done it."

The next day, the young woman decided to ask her mom about the recipe. She replied, "That is how your grandma always did it, and I learned the recipe from her." The answer didn't satisfy the young woman, so she called her grandma and asked her the same question: "Why do you cut the ends off the roast before you prepare it?"

The grandmother thought for a while, since it had been years since she made the roast herself, and then said, "The roast was always bigger than the pan I had back then. I could only make it fit by cutting the ends off."

What does this story have to do with preparing yourself for hardships in life? As we stop questioning why things are done the way they're done, we confine ourselves to blind obedience. There's no growth—neither personal growth nor comfort zone growth—when we stop seeking new perspectives, asking questions, and pushing the envelope. We become creatures of habit, limiting ourselves to what's familiar and safe instead of exposing ourselves to new ideas.

And what is mental resilience if not the ability to adapt to changing circumstances? This is why I consider it so important to welcome new ideas and perspectives in life. This is why it's so important to teach children why something is done the way it's done, instead of just saying "because I say so." This is why it pays to stop and think before you follow yet another unwritten rule; question if it makes sense first.

Traveling is an excellent exercise in opening yourself to new views and customs. Talking with people who have different opinions and live different lifestyles than you do is also valuable. So is periodically changing your mind and testing a different approach than the one you've been following for a long time.

For example, I questioned my belief that you can only become fit by going to the gym. Subsequently, I discovered that you can still be in shape even when you stay away from gym equipment. Now, even when I don't have access to a proper gym, I can still have a good workout.

A person who blindly follows all the rules, traditions, and societal expectations will inevitably end up not only unhappy, but also unable to adapt to a different world. Questioning dogmas and doing things the opposite way will continuously expand your mind and help you become more flexible and better prepared to deal with unforeseen hardships.

Destroying Your Self-Image

Don't worry, I don't mean anything reckless or dangerous by that. By destroying your self-image, I mean opening yourself to experiences that don't match your personality, your worldview, your background, or your status in society.

It doesn't have to be anything extreme, anything you hate—an introvert doesn't need to go to a night club, and an extrovert doesn't need to sign up for a weeklong silent meditation retreat (though it could be an eye-opening experience for both of them). Instead, it's about learning new skills, starting new projects, and exposing yourself to things you've always stayed away from because you assumed a person like you couldn't or shouldn't do them.

For example, as an introvert I shouldn't have attended conferences with dozens of people. Yet I did—and learned a lot about myself as I voluntarily put myself in an uncomfortable environment.

As a person without an academic background in psychology, I shouldn't have written any self-help books. Yet I did—and I'm happy to report that my perspective of a regular guy sharing his thoughts about self-discipline has resonated with thousands of people all over the world.

As a person who doesn't understand and doesn't enjoy most forms of visual arts, I still try to periodically expose myself to them. I'll admit, I'm usually so confused I don't get much out of it, but confusion is a sign that you're expanding your comfort zone. I might never become an expert in painting and enjoy it as much as a person well-versed in it, but at least I can still challenge myself as I try to decipher it.

Destroying your self-image can even be as simple as trying foods you've always stayed away from, maybe because of a childhood trauma or just that they never appealed to you. I used to hate tomatoes with a passion. Now I love them. A whole new world opened to me when I decided to stop defining myself as a person who hates tomatoes. Greek salad is now on my menu at least a few times a month.

A good sign that you've been growing is that you do things that you would have never imagined yourself doing a few years ago. Take a few minutes to see how many such changes you've experienced in the past few years. If you're struggling to find them, it's time to destroy your self-image now.

Suffer a Little Today to Suffer Less Tomorrow

Over half a year later after that fateful phone call, I woke up in the middle of the night to a fire raging across the vacant lot right in front of my house. It threatened to enter my backyard and burn everything in it, if not reach the residence as well. A swift response from firefighters ensured that nobody was hurt and no property other than some bush on the vacant plot was destroyed.

Despite the harrowing experience of waking up in the middle of the night to a fire, the next day I laughed it off. What happened in September set such a high threshold that few things will ever provoke an emotional response of a similar magnitude.

Likewise, all of the voluntary types of suffering I exposed myself to—exotic travels, some dangerous adventures, extreme sports, and facing my fears head on—helped me to better handle unwanted tribulations. Through suffering a little today, on your own terms, and in a controlled environment, you may possibly suffer less tomorrow. And this is the most important message of this chapter, one you will be grateful to heed as you go through life.

I do not wish a tragedy on anyone, but the sad truth is that it does happen to someone each day. Countless misfortunes befall millions of people around the globe. It's naïve to assume that we'll never endure agony from unforeseen hardships. But if voluntary suffering can prepare you to stay just a tiny bit calmer as a nightmare scenario comes true, you'll be glad you took the time and effort to practice it today. Don't you agree?

PREPARING FOR FUTURE CHALLENGES: QUICK RECAP

1. You can prepare yourself for future challenges by expanding your comfort zone, a psychological state in which you feel at peace and in control. This comes down to exposing yourself to things that might be scary, uncomfortable, or otherwise unfamiliar to you.

2. The first way to grow your comfort zone is through experiencing extreme mental states. You can accomplish that through fasting, exposing yourself to extreme temperatures, facing your fears, and subjecting yourself to voluntary everyday discomfort.

3. Questioning dogmas and exposing yourself to new perspectives is another way to grow your comfort zone and become better at adapting yourself to new situations, including unplanned hardships.

4. Destroying your self-image by doing things that aren't your cup of tea is yet another way to stretch your comfort zone. A good sign that you've been growing is that you're doing things that you

would have never imagined yourself engaging with a few years ago.

5. As you let in some voluntary suffering today, you'll raise the level of intensity of hardships you can manage without breaking down. Through some voluntary practice now, you can diminish the impact of future unplanned, unpleasant circumstances.

Chapter 5: On Helping Those Whose Worlds Were Rocked to the Core

Over many years spent following the personal development world, I've grown to hate certain catchphrases. One of those: "You're the average of the five people you spend the most time with." There's a dangerous implication in this statement: if one of your friends is struggling with a crisis, it's best to stay away, lest they "infect" you with their hardships, too.

Of course, not everyone is so heartless and success-oriented as to believe this adage to a T, yet there exists a certain tendency to shun "losers"—as if they wanted to struggle and suffer. Granted, certain people do sentence themselves to inevitable hardships through bad choices. However, the vast majority don't—adversity is often random in nature, and as such, if any of our friends fall victim to it, we should do our best to support rather than stay away.

In the last chapter of this book, I would like to offer some suggestions on how to help others whose worlds have turned upside down. It seems like a simple topic, yet I've come to realize there's a certain art to it, certain good practices and certain bad ones that should be avoided at all cost. Let's discuss them with a brief do and do not list.

Do Empathize. Do Not Judge.

What is a life-changing crisis for one person might not be a big deal for another. Sometimes, the only reason why we can't understand why our friend is freaking out so much is because we aren't in their shoes; any problem seen from the outside is less terrifying than when we experience it ourselves. This is why it's so important to empathize with a person who's suffering, but never to judge their emotional response. Avoid comparing their struggles to yours in a way that would make them feel as if you're telling them how they should feel or that they should do things differently.

Never judge another person's hardships based on your own standards. Yes, you might have survived fifteen heartbreaks by the time you were twenty and feel fine, but your friend might not be so resilient. Their own heartbreak is a big deal for them, and your dismissal or suggestion that they're overreacting doesn't help. In fact, it makes things worse for them. Feel their pain. Try to see the problem from their own eyes, not yours. And never, ever belittle their problems.

Do Tell the Truth. Do Not Offer Cheap Platitudes.

When someone's life turns upside down and a big crisis threatens their normal way of living, it is not the time for cheap, generalized statements to soothe them, no matter how well-intentioned.

It's tempting to console, to offer hope for the future, or to try to make the problem appear smaller than it is. However, ultimately, what a friend needs in the immediate aftermath of a catastrophe is acknowledgment of their pain. Don't be afraid to say that the situation sucks—this is infinitely better and more helpful than saying "keep your head up" to a defeated person who may barely be able to get out of bed.

Don't go overboard with your frankness, though: this is about acknowledging what the other person is feeling, not torturing them with additional implications they may not have thought about.

Do Offer Support in Recovery. Do Not Fix Unless Asked.

As a person interested in personal development, you may have a tendency to jump straight into solutions. However, this doesn't work for a person dealing with a big crisis. In that case, the obstacles seem so insurmountable that they need time to process what happened and create some distance (as explained in Chapters 1 and 2) before they're ready to get into problem-solving mode.

Trying to fix a bad situation when you haven't been asked to is equal to rushing the suffering person into recovery. And if there's one thing about recovery, it's that it cannot be rushed. You don't want your friend to make difficult decisions when they're under too much pressure and can't think with a clear head yet. Help them prioritize self-care.

Do Keep Your Promises. Do Not Offer Empty Ones.

If you offer your friend help, be specific with what you can and can't do. Don't forget to be specific regarding when you're available to help. It sounds obvious to say that you're available 24/7, but ask yourself if you're *really* prepared to get up in the middle of the night to talk with your friend in pain. If not, don't make empty promises. You aren't necessarily a bad person if you can't be there for them literally all the time—the most important thing is to be there for them when you can.

No matter what you promise, keep your word at all costs. There's nothing worse than being in pain and gathering the courage to reach out to a friend, only for them to not keep their word. Be reliable and specific regarding what you can offer, even if you can only check on your friend once a week for a few minutes.

Do Keep in Touch. Do Not Stay Away to Give Them Space Unless Asked.

When your friend is in pain, it's tempting to tell them, "Let me know when you need something" and then disappear, assuming that when they need you, they'll let you know. Nothing is farther from the truth.

A person trying to make sense of a difficult situation may be incapable of gathering the courage to reach out to you. They may fear that they're asking for too much, that they're bothering you, or they may decide that it's better to suffer alone even though they'd love to face their hardships with a friendly face.

Periodically check on your friend, even if it's just a quick message asking how they feel. Don't immediately assume that they aren't interested in hanging out, that you should stay away until they feel "better," or that they don't want to see you—unless they specifically tell you to give them some space.

When reaching out, extend specific offers: even if your friend is hurting, they may still want to go have coffee with you, they may still appreciate you bringing a cake, or they may still want to enjoy a moment of normalcy as you cook something together. Don't force them to tell you what they'd like to do— provide ideas yourself. Even if they say no, they'll appreciate your initiative.

ON HELPING THOSE WHOSE WORLDS WERE ROCKED TO THE CORE: QUICK RECAP

1. When a friend is struggling with adversity, don't stay away in fear that misfortune will choose you next. Offer support.

2. Don't judge your friend's pain or dismiss it, even if you have rich personal experience facing similar hardships. Empathize instead. Feel their pain. Try to see the problem from their own eyes, not yours.

3. It's better to acknowledge to your friend that their situation sucks rather than offer cheap platitudes that may aggravate them. Tell the truth, not comforting lies.

4. Help your friend prioritize self-care over encouraging them to fix the problem right away. They're not in the right state of mind, no matter how great you think your solutions are.

5. Be specific with what you can and can't do for your friend, and keep your word. If you offer help, be reliable and don't back out of your promises.

6. Don't disappear assuming that your friend will reach out when they need you. Give them space if they ask you to do so, but if not, periodically check on them and extend your specific offers for help.

Epilogue

We can't ever be prepared for everything that life throws at us. I wasn't prepared at all for that phone call in September and the sudden loss of a loved one (who was such a great support for so many people). Neither was I—nor virtually anyone else on the planet—ready for an unprecedented global health crisis. Sadly, the most incomprehensible things happen to people every day, and one day these things might happen to us, too.

Each hardship can teach us something valuable. But as I emphasized in the first chapter, even with a long-term perspective, we won't be able to consider every single crisis we suffer in life as something that was "good" for us. There's nothing good in losing a loved one. To even suggest so is blasphemous.

The main focus of this book was thus on crises that, while still possibly excruciating, can be mitigated and eventually turned into blessings in disguise. We've learned that the best way to handle them is to focus on self-care and self-understanding rather than self-guilt and self-harm. Only when we manage to put some distance between the problem and ourselves can we make cool-headed decisions that will help us recover and eventually bounce back.

Lastly, to emerge stronger and achieve at least partial immunity against future hardships, we need to inject into our everyday lives a speck of voluntary suffering. We can't create a problem-free life. What we can do, however, is train ourselves to handle problems better when they do appear. Sometimes, they'll just slightly tilt our worlds, and sometimes they'll turn things upside down. Ultimately, mental resilience is our only tool to keep going when it seems it's not worth it anymore.

Thank You for Reading— Don't Forget Your Gift

Don't forget your free book as thanks for buying this one. Here's where you can get it:

https://www.profoundselfimprovement.com/dt

Could You Help?

I'd love to hear your opinion about my book. In the world of publishing, there are few things more valuable than honest reviews from a wide variety of readers. Your review not only helps me, but also fellow readers who rely on ratings to decide whether a given book is worth their investment.

About Martin Meadows

Martin Meadows is a bestselling personal development author, writing about self-discipline and its transformative power to help you become successful and live a more fulfilling life. With a straight-to-the point approach, he is passionate about sharing tips, habits, and resources for self-improvement through a combination of science-backed research and personal experience.

Embracing self-control helped Martin overcome extreme shyness, build successful businesses, learn multiple languages, become a bestselling author, and more. As a lifelong learner, he enjoys exploring the limits of his comfort zone through often extreme experiments and adventures involving various sports and wild or exotic places.

Martin uses a pen name. It helps him focus on serving his readers through writing, without the distractions of seeking recognition. He doesn't believe in branding himself as an infallible expert (which he is not), opting instead to offer suggestions and solutions as a fellow personal growth experimenter, with all of the associated failures and successes.

You can read more of his books here: http://www.amazon.com/author/martinmeadows.